Speakeasy Activities 3e

A2 / B1

Coordination pédagogique de l'ouvrage :
Ruth Alimi
IA-IPR, Académie de Créteil

Avec la contribution de :
Marie-Christine Delsinne
Collège Denecourt, Bois-le-Roi (77)
Formatrice, Académie de Créteil

Christophe Goarant-Corrêa-de-Sá
Formateur, Académie d'Orléans-Tours

Alison Bouhmid
PRAG, Université Paul Valéry, Montpellier 3

Maider Chena Basanta

Anna Guill
Collège l'Ardillière de Nézant, Saint-Brice-sous-Forêt (95)
Formatrice, Académie de Versailles

Antony McDermott
École Jeannine Manuel, Paris (75)

Patrick Santoro
Lycée Pierre-Gilles de Gennes, Paris (75)

Pascal Vinson
Collège Pilâtre de Rozier, Paris (75)
Formateur, Académie de Paris

Jennifer Wattrelot
Collège Renée Taillefer, Gaillac (81)

Nathan

La 3e est la 3e année du cycle 4 instauré par les nouveaux programmes de la réforme des collèges applicables à partir de la rentrée 2016. Ce cycle regroupe les classes de 5e, 4e et 3e.

En anglais LV1, en fin de cycle 4, tous les élèves doivent avoir atteint le niveau A2 dans les 5 activités langagières et le niveau visé est B1 dans plusieurs activités langagières. En anglais LV2, en fin de cycle 4, le niveau visé est A2 dans au moins deux activités langagières.

Activité langagière	ÉCOUTER ET COMPRENDRE (MP3)	LIRE	RÉAGIR ET DIALOGUER	PARLER EN CONTINU	ÉCRIRE ET RÉAGIR À L'ÉCRIT
A1	Peut comprendre des mots familiers et des expressions courantes sur lui-même, sa famille et son environnement.	Peut comprendre, des textes courts et très simples, phrase par phrase, en relevant des noms, des mots familiers et des expressions très élémentaires et en relisant si nécessaire.	Peut interagir brièvement dans des situations déjà connues en utilisant des mots et expressions simples et avec un débit lent.	Peut produire des expressions simples, isolées, sur les gens et les choses.	Peut écrire des expressions et phrases simples isolées.
A2	Peut comprendre une intervention brève si elle est claire et simple.	Peut comprendre de courts textes simples sur des sujets concrets courants avec une fréquence élevée de langue quotidienne.	Peut interagir avec une aisance raisonnable dans des situations bien structurées et de courtes conversations à condition que le locuteur apporte de l'aide le cas échéant.	Peut décrire ou présenter simplement des gens, des conditions de vie, des activités quotidiennes, ce qu'on aime ou pas, par de courtes séries d'expressions ou de phrases.	Peut écrire une série d'expressions et de phrases simples reliées par des connecteurs simples tels que « et », «mais» et « parce que ».
B1	Peut comprendre une information factuelle sur des sujets simples en distinguant l'idée générale et les points de détail, à condition que l'articulation soit claire et l'accent courant.	Peut lire des textes factuels directs sur des sujets relatifs à son domaine et à ses intérêts avec un niveau satisfaisant de compréhension.	Peut exprimer un avis, manifester un sentiment et donner quelques éléments simples de contexte sur un sujet abstrait ou culturel.	Peut assez aisément mener à bien une description directe et non compliquée de sujets variés dans son domaine en la présentant comme une succession linéaire de points.	Peut écrire un énoncé simple et bref sur des sujets familiers ou déjà connus.

Les trois parcours des nouveaux programmes

Dans les nouveaux programmes, les apprentissages s'inscrivent dans **3 parcours** qui donnent du sens aux apprentissages :

Le parcours citoyen Parcours citoyen fait des élèves des personnes responsables.

Le parcours artistique Parcours artistique sensibilise les élèves à toutes les formes d'art.

Le parcours avenir Parcours avenir permet de préparer son orientation professionnelle.

Édition : Seonaid Cruickshank, assistée de Margot Pastier
Iconographie : Nathalie Bencal
Illustrateurs : Nicolas Paillard de Chesnay, Claude-Henri Saunier
Conception de la maquette : Frédéric Jely
Mise en page : Domino
Conception de la couverture : Frédéric Jély

ISBN 978.2.09.174153.6

Sommaire

Pistes EPI - Croisements entre enseignements

Certaines séquences pourront servir de base à la conception et à la mise en place d'un EPI (Enseignement pratique interdisciplinaire) :

Séquence ***Volunteering in the Peace Corps*** EPI 6 thématique : Langues et cultures étrangères
• Croisement possible avec le programme de 3e d'**EMC** sur le thème : L'engagement : agir individuellement et collectivement.
• Croisement possible avec le programme de 3e d'**histoire** sur le thème 2 : Le monde depuis 1945.

Séquence ***Windrush Generation*** EPI 6 thématique : Langues et cultures étrangères
• Croisement possible avec le programme de 3e d'**EMC** sur le thème : L'engagement : agir individuellement et collectivement.
• Croisement possible avec le programme de 3e d'**histoire** sur le thème 2: Le monde depuis 1945.

Séquence ***Building Europe*** EPI 4 thématique : Information, communication, citoyenneté
• Croisement possible avec le programme de 3e d'**EMC** sur le thème : L'engagement : agir individuellement et collectivement.
• Croisement possible avec le programme de 3e d'**histoire** sur le thème 2: Le monde depuis 1945.

Séquence ***War Horse*** EPI 6 thématique : Langues et cultures étrangères
• Croisement possible avec le programme de 3e d'**histoire** sur le thème 1 : L'Europe, un théâtre majeur des guerres totales (1914-1945).
• Croisement possible avec le programme de 3e de **français** sur le thème : Se chercher, se construire.

Getting Work Experience

Activity 1 An Interview with the School's Careers Counsellor

Group A Do Activity 1 on this page. **Group B** Your Activity 1 is on page 74.

Amber Jones, a student at Richmond School, wants to become a chef. She meets with the school's careers counsellor to ask him questions and advice about her project. Work in two groups to get ready to role-play the interview.

Group A: You are Amber.

A Get ready to answer questions about yourself.

Name: Amber Jones

Age: 15

Class: Year 10

Hobbies: cooking – a passion since age 8 – as often as possible

Subjects for GCSE*: English, Maths, Sciences, History ☹, Religious Studies, French, Food Technology ☺ and Food and Nutrition

Career aspiration: becoming a chef

Words

GCSE: General Certificate of Secondary Education – an exam taken by many British students at age 16

B Talking about your personality.

1. **Select the four adjectives you find most important for a chef – discuss your selection as a group and be prepared to give your reasons.**

patient • creative • generous • stubborn (= you don't change your mind or accept criticism) • able to work in a team • reliable (= people can trust you) • fast • precise • autonomous • clean • obedient (= you do what you are told) • tidy

2. **Get ready to describe yourself using those four adjectives and to explain why they are important and should help you in your project.**

C Prepare some questions you want to ask about the job.

Salary? • Working hours? • Studies? • Length of the studies? • Amount of women doing the job? • Chances to get a job?

D Ask for some advice about what to do.

go into apprenticeship after GCSEs • work during the holidays • find a part-time job after class • do training periods in restaurants • do the school's work experience week in a kitchen

Should I...? What should I...? Would you recommend to...? Is it a good idea to...? How can I...?

E Pair up with someone from the other group and practise your interview for five minutes. Get ready to perform it in front of the class.

@ CONNECT TO: collegien.nathan.fr/speak3 to discover other careers.

Activity 2 Amber's Phone Call for a Work-Experience Placement

Learn as You Wish

Listen to the conversation and fill in the mind map, or answer the questions. Choose the method you prefer, A or B.

A Listen to the conversation and take notes:

person Amber speaks to?

her work placement request?

thing(s) she needs doing next?

work placement conditions?

important rules in kitchens?

Amber's skills as a cook?

B If you are not so confident, answer the following questions.

1. What type of business is Amber phoning?

....

2. Person she speaks to? ....

3. Now concentrate on Amber's answers.

a. Dates for Amber's work placement? ....

b. Amber wants to do it: ☐ in the kitchen ☐ serving

c. Reason why? ....

d. Things that she enjoys cooking at the moment?

☐ gazpacho ☐ artichoke soup ☐ tiramisu ☐ whole almond sauce ☐ hollandaise sauce

4. What's next?

a. Thing Amber needs to do? ....

b. Person she should meet? ....

5. If she gets the work placement, Amber:

a. ☐ will be able to cook meals. ☐ won't be able to cook meals.

b. ☐ will mainly observe. ☐ will do things in the kitchen.

c. ☐ will have some freedom. ☐ will have to do exactly what she is told.

6. Name of the man? ....

Get ready to recap information and sum up the conversation.

Activity 3 Writing Amber's Letter

Use this model letter to write Amber's application letter for a work placement (you can invent addresses).

Your name
Full address
Town postcode
Phone number

The employers' name
Full address
Town postcode

Date: ....

Dear Person's name or Sir or Madam,

I would like to enquire about the possibility of a work-experience placement with your company for a week, from the .... to the ....

I am (age) and a student at (school name).

I am in (school year).

I would like to work (at your company / in a shop / in your school...) because ....

I have (list any experience that you may have e.g. do babysitting for friends/ family, have a part time job in a local shop...)

I am (list some of your personal skills and qualities e.g. *friendly, reliable, hard working, enjoy meeting people*, etc). My personal interests are (write any that may help with your application).

I look forward to hearing from you.

Yours sincerely (or Yours faithfully)

(Sign your letter)
Print your name

TIPS

If you started your letter Dear Sir or Madam, finish with "Yours faithfully".
If you started Dear (person's name), finish with "Yours sincerely".

Activity 4 Safety Regulations in the Kitchen

A **Amber got her work experience at Claire's Brasserie. Claire, the chef, welcomes her and tells her about safety regulations in the kitchen.**
Sort out what Amber MUST – MUSTN'T or CAN'T – CAN do.
Put the correct word in each blank:

1. .... do things without asking first.

2. .... wash hands regularly.

3. .... ask questions whenever necessary.

4. .... help people if they offer.

5. .... touch hot boiling pans.

6. .... obey immediately.

7. .... wear a hat or fasten your hair with an elastic band.

TIPS

What other modals can you use as well as must and can? Match the modals in the first column with their equivalents in the second column.

	• be allowed to
must •	• be forbidden to
mustn't •	• have to
can •	• be able to
can't •	• not be allowed to
	• be unable to / not be able to

B **Complete with appropriate modals or their equivalents.**

1. Yesterday I .... help the sous-chef to prepare a sauce. Claire gave me permission.

2. At home, I .... cook the same dishes as in a restaurant. I don't have the appropriate utensils.

3. Next week, I .... meet the careers counsellor again. The school insists on it when the work placement is finished.

4. Claire is a great creative chef. She .... prepare many different things, from main courses to desserts.

5. Safety is very important in a kitchen. That's why you .... forget to follow the rules.

Your Task

Work Placement Log Book

Her school asked Amber to keep a log book of her daily activities during the work placement. Complete what she wrote after her first day at Claire's Brasserie. Give the reasons.

Today was my first day at Claire's Brasserie.

I had to ....

And I wasn't allowed to ....

But I was allowed to ....

So I was able to ....

Learn as You Wish

Choose the method you prefer, A or B, to help you remember what you have learned.

A Without looking back at the previous activities, can you:

1. List some questions you revised in this unit.

....

....

2. List some useful expressions to use in an application letter.

....

....

3. List some vocabulary related to kitchens.

....

....

Then look back at the previous pages and see if there is anything more you can add.

B Look back at the previous activities and:

1. List some questions you revised in this unit.

....

....

2. List some useful expressions to use in an application letter.

....

....

3. List some vocabulary related to kitchens.

....

....

....

Elementary, My Dear Watson!

Activity 1 Introducing Sherlock

A What do you know about the fictional characters Sherlock Holmes and Dr Watson?

1. Type of stories: ....

2. Country: ....

3. Time: ☐ 18th century ☐ 19th century ☐ 20th century ☐ 21st century

4. Jobs: ....

B Look at the photo, from a BBC TV series. You are going to watch an extract from the series.

1. Who do you think the characters in the photo are?

....

2. Probable time when the story is set:
☐ 18th century ☐ 19th century ☐ 20th century ☐ 21st century

C @ CONNECT TO: collegien.nathan.fr/speak3

Watch the extract with the SOUND OFF and answer:

1. Number of characters: ....

2. The place: ....

D **Watch the extract with the SOUND ON.**

1. a. What does Dr Watson say in the beginning? ....

....

b. This scene is the first time that ....

2. Listen carefully for these keywords and use them to recap what Sherlock Holmes deduced about Dr Watson.

army • doctor • Afghanistan • brother • alcoholic • wife

....

3. Imagine the questions Dr Watson has about this strange character after this scene.

....

....

Activity 2 Listening to an Interview

MP3 **Listen to the recording.**

A **Take notes about 221b Baker Street.**

....

....

B **Inspiration for Sherlock Holmes.**

1. Select the appropriate answer:

☐ Only Sherlock Holmes is based on Sir Arthur Conan Doyle himself.

☐ Both Sherlock Holmes and Dr Watson are based on Sir Arthur Conan Doyle.

☐ Only Dr Watson is based on Sir Arthur Conan Doyle himself.

2. Who was Dr Joseph Bell? Pick out keywords and recap.

....

....

C **Dr Bell's diagnosis method.**

1. He could .... and decide whether ....

....

2. He could tell from ....

what ☐ grade ☐ trade he had.

3. Deduce the meaning of the word you selected: ....

4. This sort of thing was .... at the time than today.

5. Because these days, whatever your job is, you ....

Activity 3 Sherlock Holmes Webquest

Group A Do Activity 3 on this page.

Group B Your Activity is on page 75.

Group A

A @ CONNECT TO: collegien.nathan.fr/speak3

Go to the website, take notes using the following spidergram and get ready to answer the other group's questions about Sir Arthur Conan Doyle.

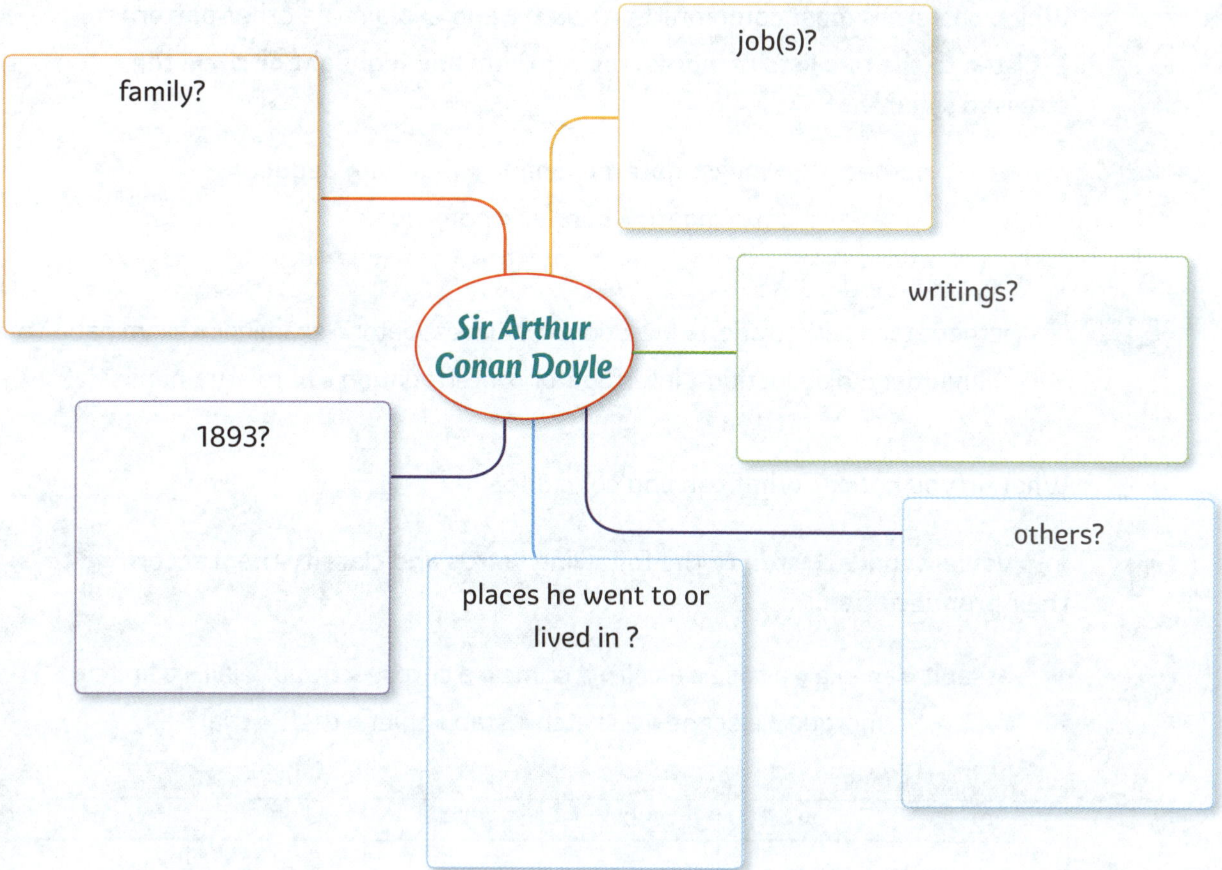

B **Get ready to ask the other group questions about Joseph Bell:**

1. Period when he lived? ....

2. Reasons for fame: At the time? / Today?

....

3. Job(s)? ....

4. Person he was influenced by? ....

5. Examples of his deductions? ....

6. People's reaction? ....

7. Impact on his practice as a doctor? ....

Learn as You Wish

To practise your speaking skills, choose the method you prefer, A or B.

MP3 **A** **1. Word stress. Listen to the following words and highlight or circle the stressed syllable. Repeat them several times.**

motive • police • station • precinct • witness • private • burglar • murder • rifle • shoplift • blackmail • body • strangle • poison • footprint • prison • handgun

How many of these different stress patterns did you hear? □●• □●● □•● □••?
Which pattern is most common? Can you try and explain the other patterns?

2. Listen to the two lists of words, repeat them and highlight or circle the stressed syllable.

MP3 **a.** perpetrate • investigate • examine • murder • deduct • interrogate • burglar • homicide

MP3 **b.** perpetrator • perpetration • investigation • investigator • examiner • examination • murderer • deduction • interrogator • interrogation • burglary • homicidal

What do you notice? What can you conclude?

MP3 **B** **Vowel sounds. Listen to the following words and classify them according to their pronunciation.**

assault • an axe • a case • a cell • a crime • a corpse • fraud • jail • a knife • morgue • a scene • a sketch • stab • thief • theft • trial

eɪ	aɪ	iː	ɔː	æ	e

Activity 4 What Were They Doing?

Professor Bell enters his classroom and observes his students attentively. He immediately deduces what six of the students were doing before he arrived. What about you ?

Activity 5 Learning and Pronouncing Crime Vocabulary

A **Match the following words to their phonetic transcriptions. Do you know what each word means?**

footprints

blood

kluːz

/naɪf/

blʌd

knife

ˈwepən

ˈbɒdɪ

clues

ˌdiːenˈeɪ

ˈfʊtprɪnts

weapon

body

DNA

B **Match the following words to their definitions.**

1. alibi /'ælɪbaɪ/ •
2. crime scene /kraɪm siːn/ •
3. evidence /'evɪdəns/ •
4. suspect /'sʌspɛkt/ •
5. witness /'wɪtnɪs/ •

• **a.** A person who saw a crime happen.
• **b.** Where you were and who you were with at the time of a crime.
• **c.** A person who has a motive to commit a crime.
• **d.** The place where a crime was committed.
• **e.** A detail or a fact that proves a point and helps the police.

Your Task

Role-playing a Detective Story

A **Read this police report about Lord Spencer's death:**

January 23

Lord John Spencer was found stabbed in the kitchen of his manor. Forensic Doctor Joseph Bell estimates he died at 8:30 pm. Traces of blood were found all through the kitchen from the garden door into the living room. The door was locked from the inside. No windows were broken. Both a large sum of money and Lady Spencer's jewellery are missing.
Mr Edward Higgins, Lord Spencer's lawyer, discovered the body at 9 pm with Jonathan Hopkins, Lord Spencer's secretary, who had just returned from the cinema.
Mr Higgins had an appointment with Lord Spencer, who wanted to change his will.
Emma Thompson, the maid, and the butler, Jeremy Green, were present in the manor but didn't hear anything.
Some people think Mr Green was having an affair with Lady Spencer and it was well-known that Lord Spencer was about to dismiss Miss Thompson.
Lady Spencer was so shocked she couldn't be interviewed.

B **In small groups, list the suspects and give their motives.**

C **Study the role card your teacher gave you, get ready to impersonate your character and interact with the others.**

Volunteering in the Peace Corps

Activity 1 What Does the Peace Corps Do?

You are going to find out about an organisation called the Peace Corps. But first, what do you imagine it could be? Match the missions in the list with the organisation you think does them, and complete with your own ideas:

fight • give medication • win battles • drop bombs • build hospitals • make prisoners • raise money • restore peace and maintain order • teach • use guns • protect civilian populations

1. The Armed Forces:

2. The Peace Corps:

Learn as You Wish

Keeping track of everything you learn. Choose the method you prefer, A or B.

A Write a recap of what you have understood about the Peace Corps so far. These prompts can help you.

So far, I've learned that ....

I have understood that the difference between .... and .... is ....

It seems that some of the missions of .... are ....

B Use a KWL chart (can you guess what KWL stands for?). For now, you can start filling in the first two columns. You can fill in more as you do more activities.

What I KNOW about the Peace Corps	What I WANT to know about the Peace Corps	What I LEARNED about the Peace Corps

Activity 2 Listening to an Interview

A **Listen to Megan Larson Koné, and in groups of 2 or 3, answer the following questions with short sentences.**

MP3

1. Who are the Peace Corps members?

....

2. Where do they work?

....

3. When did they first appear?

....

B **The Peace Corps has 3 objectives. Complete this mind map with the words you have picked out with your group.**

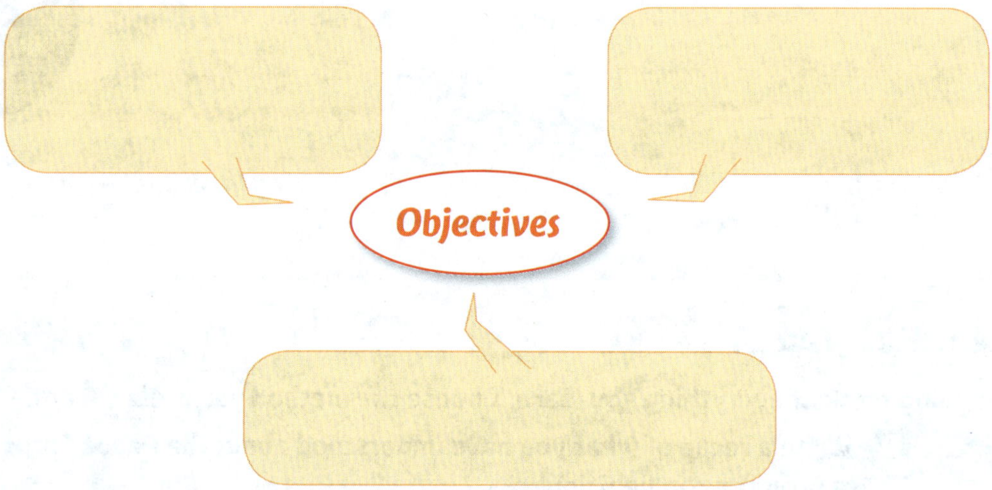

C **1.** Write down the repeated words you recognise:

....

2. Write down other words you recognise:

....

Learn as You Wish

A **Write a recap of what you have understood about the Peace Corps so far. These prompts can help you.**

In Activity 1, I found out that ....

But now thanks to Activity 2, I have learned ....

I wanted to know .... and now ....

I didn't imagine that ....

Now I know more about ....

B **Fill in column three on the KWL chart you started on page 15.**

Activity 3 Volunteering in Côte d'Ivoire

MP3 **A Listen to Megan Larson-Koné.**

1. Underline her tasks in Côte d'Ivoire.

work on water and sanitation • make the local community understand hiv and aids • give injections • teach business skills • help build houses • work in the fields • open a cooperative

2. Now answer these questions.

a. When and where did Megan work as a Peace Corps volunteer?

b. Who did Megan work with?

c. What were the aims of the programme?

B Listen to the passage again.

a. Pick out words ending in *-tion* and circle the syllable with the main stress.

b. Do the same with words ending in *-ity*.

C Now get ready to orally recap what you know about the programme and about how Megan and her volunteer group worked. You may use the prompts provided in Activity 1 and Activity 2 Pay special attention to stress, rhythm and pronunciation. Use this model to organise your recap so you do not have to read notes.

A few facts about Megan and her involvement with the Peace Corps (When, where, ...):

What her mission consisted of (tasks, partners, aims):

Activity 4 Origins of the Peace Corps

@ CONNECT TO: collegien.nathan.fr/speak3

A Log on to the website. Read the text down to "freedom".

1. When he had the idea of the Peace Corps, John Fitzgerald Kennedy:

☐ was president. ☐ was running for presidency.

2. What did JFK want to encourage?

....

3. What did he ask young Americans to do?

☐ Stay in the U.S. ☐ Work in the Foreign Service. ☐ Travel around the world for fun.

☐ Travel to developing countries.

4. Which two causes did he expect them to dedicate themselves to?

....

5. Find a synonym for "give their time to". ....

6. According to JFK, the Soviet Union had hundreds of volunteers abroad. What for?

....

7. What made JFK create the Peace Corps?

....

....

8. Pick out elements showing that Kennedy's idea received warm public support.

B **Read the final paragraph – "The Peace Corps Today".**

What has changed? What is still the same?

Activity 5 Pairwork: Checking Comprehension

MP3 **A** **Listen to the whole interview again. Find the name of Megan's programme.**

B **Read the whole worksheet again and ask your partner questions to make sure he/she understood what the Peace Corps is and what Megan's experience was about.**

Your Task

A Volunteer Programme Competition

A **The Peace Corps Agency has organised a project competition. In groups of four, get ready to present and defend your project.**

Create a PowerPoint document to present your project and comment on it orally. Don't read notes. You may organise your ideas in a mind map:

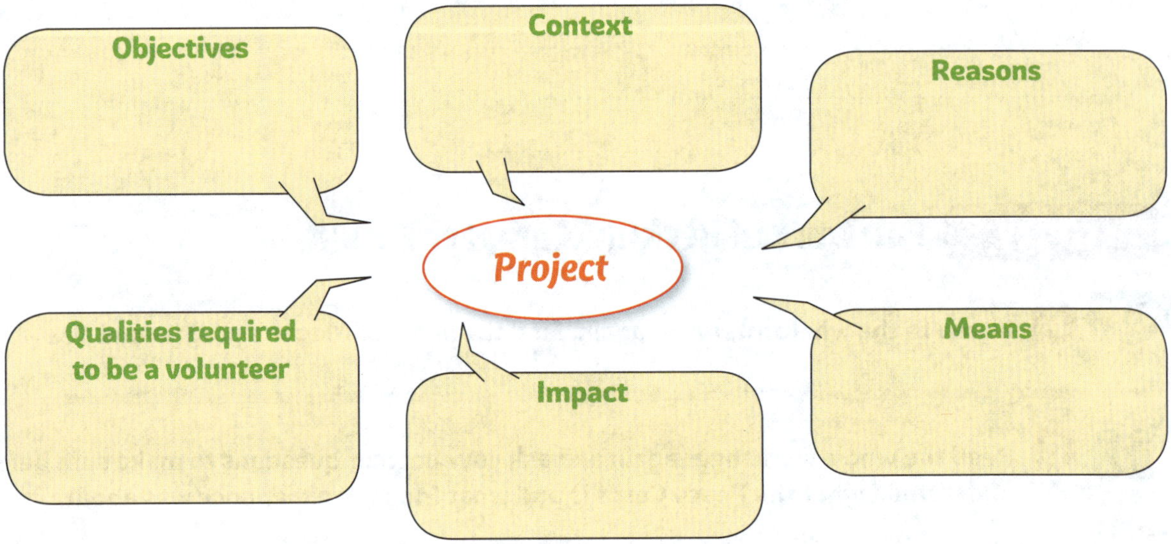

TIPS

If you need ideas for projects @ CONNECT TO: *collegien.nathan.fr/speak3*

B **Decide on the winning programme.**

1. Take a few notes during the presentations. Concentrate on the following aspects:

The project (missions, ideas, etc.)

Language (varied vocabulary, grammar, comprehensibility)

The presentation (PowerPoint, body language, eye contact and conviction)

2. Discuss the presentations and decide on the winning programme.

The Globe Theatre

Activity 1 William Shakespeare

Group A Do Activity 1 on this page. Group B Your Activity 1 is on page 76.

Group A

@ CONNECT TO: collegien.nathan.fr/speak3

A Click on the entry: "Who was Shakespeare?" and find:

1. Birthdate? .... **2.** Birthplace? ....

3. Date of death? ....

4. Family life? ....

5. Famous for? ....

B Click on: "Shakespeare, the playwright". Write the three genres of his plays, and give an example for each genre. ....

....

C Click on: "Did Shakespeare really exist?" and be ready to explain the mystery about Shakespeare to the class.

D Get ready to tell the other group about Shakespeare, and to take notes about their presentation.

Learn as You Wish

1. How to make your presentation interesting.
In the following list of dos and don'ts, tick what you think you should do if you want your classmates to listen carefully to what you're going to tell them:

☐ Speak very loudly. ☐ Do not speak too loudly. ☐ Speak very slowly.
☐ Start with a list of facts. ☐ Start with a question or a problem to solve.
☐ Write down the new vocabulary on the board. ☐ Spell the new vocabulary.
☐ Write down the dates on the board. ☐ Do not let your classmates interrupt you.
☐ Make very long and elaborate sentences.

2. Match the dos and don'ts you chose to the justifications from this list. (Write the letters next to the sentences above).

a. When you do that, the language you use does not sound like English any more.
b. It tends to be monotonous.
c. That's up to you, it depends what kind of presentation you choose to give.
d. That's something you do when you're writing but not when you're speaking.
e. Doing that helps your classmates understand and follow.
f. When you do that, the audience tends to chat while you're speaking.
g. It creates a sort of suspense.

Activity 2 Exploring an Elizabethan Theatre

A Look at the pictures and the labels, then connect the parts of the theatre with their definitions.

A performance at Shakespeare's Globe Theatre today

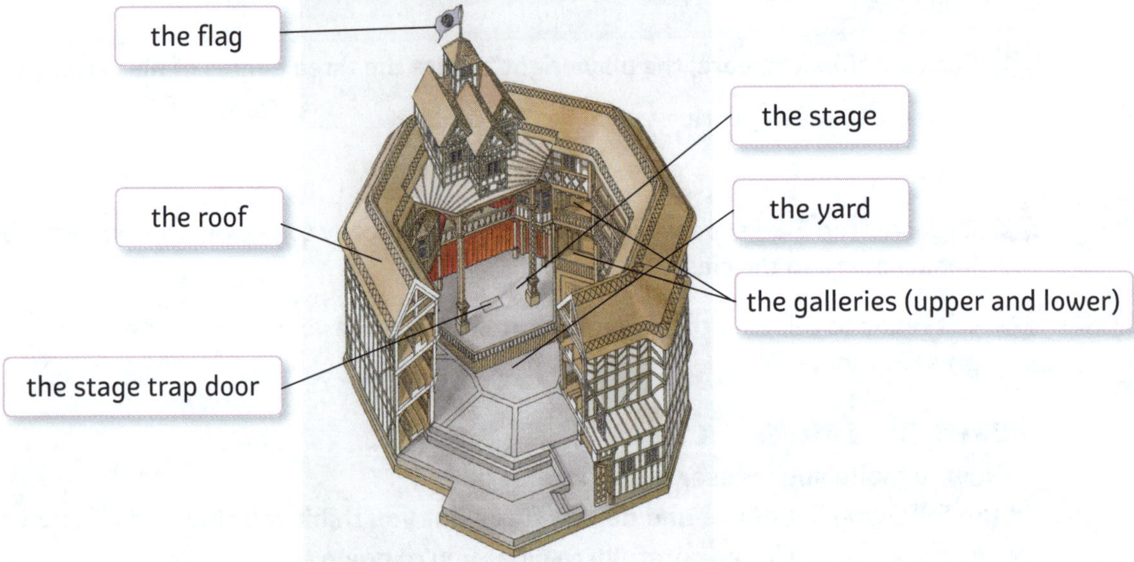

the stage •	• where the audience can sit, protected from the rain
the galleries (upper and lower) •	• when it is visible, people know a play is going to start
the yard •	• where the audience can stand, close to the actors
the roof •	• actors use it to appear or disappear
the stage trap door •	• where the actors stand
the flag •	• at the top, it protects the building from rain

B What do you notice about the theatre?

1. Roof? ....

2. Stage? ....

3. Shape? ....

Learn as you wish

Describing

Organise the following words and expressions. Choose your method, A or B.

above • around • assemble • balcony • be located • be shaped like • below • black • build • circular • columns • consist of • dark • galleries • gold • green • hexagonal • in front of • in the middle • look like • lower • musicians' gallery • next to • on the sides • platform • pointed • rectangular • red • roof • round • seats • seem to be • square • stage • stairs • structure • trap door • triangular • under • upper • white • yard = court = pit

A Complete the table.

Shapes	Localisation	Different parts	Colours	Useful verbs

B Complete the mind map as you wish.

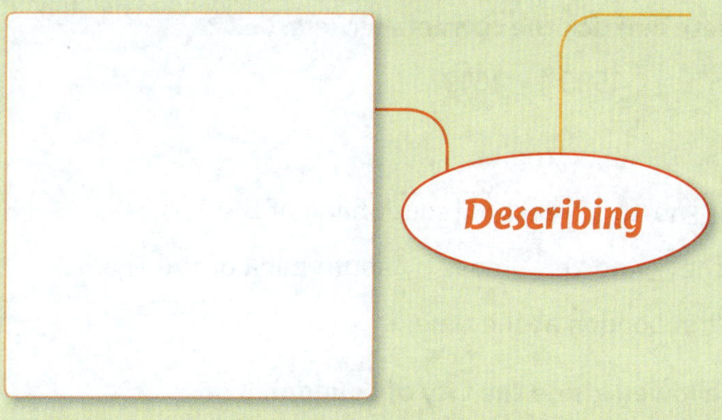

Activity 3 Theatre at the Globe

Read the following features about The Globe and link them to the consequences they implied.

- **a.** open-air theatre •
- **b.** stage with three sides •
- **c.** yard for standing spectators (called "groundlings") only •
- **d.** very little scenery or props •
- **e.** rich and poor people went to the theatre •

- • **1.** The actors had to speak very loudly.
- • **2.** The actors had to describe the setting or place.
- • **3.** The audience got wet if it rained.
- • **4.** The audience were close to the actors so they could throw things if they weren't happy!
- • **5.** Plays had to start early in the afternoon when it was still light.
- • **6.** Plays were an opportunity for all kinds of people to meet.

Activity 4 Listening to a Guide at the Globe Theatre

MP3 **A** **1. Listen to Part 1, complete and tick the correct answers.**

a. The Globe was built in ☐ 1519 ☐ 1599 ☐ 1619.

b. Monarch: ....

c. The Globe was built on the ☐ north ☐ east ☐ south bank of the Thames.

d. The City of London was on the ☐ north ☐ east ☐ south bank of the Thames.

e. The Globe ☐ was ☐ wasn't in London at the time.

2. Which activities were NOT allowed inside the City of London?

☐ gambling ☐ singing ☐ drinking alcohol ☐ riding a horse ☐ dogs killing bears

3. Popular entertainment in Shakespeare's days.

a. What animals were used: ☐ horses ☐ bears ☐ monkeys ☐ dogs ☐ bulls ☐ snakes?

b. The animals were treated ☐ well ☐ badly.

Justify by writing down one word you heard: ....

MP3 **B** **Manners and Morals. Listen to Part 2 and answer the questions below.**

1. Who went to the theatre in those days?

☐ only the rich ☐ only the poor ☐ both

2. Which adjectives does Mel use to describe the audience's behaviour?

☐ respectful ☐ disrespectful ☐ rowdy ☐ quiet ☐ noisy

3. What three things did people do at the theatre that might seem unusual to us today?

a. ....

b. ....

c. ....

4. The audience's reactions. What happened during performances? Match the elements from column A to the elements in column B.

A	B
good guys •	• go "woo!"
people kissing •	• go "boo!"
bad guys •	• cheer

Conclusion: In Shakespeare's day, the atmosphere in The Globe was similar to what happens now at .... or ....

5. The Puritans' opinions:

a. What adjective is associated with the Puritans?

☐ straight ☐ severe ☐ strict ☐ sincere

b. What words are associated to the theatre for them?

☐ lies ☐ likes ☐ moral ☐ immoral

6. Women and the theatre:

a. Who played female roles? ....

b. What adjective (question 5) can explain why women were not allowed to act in theatres?

....

Activity 5 Recapping and Contrasting

Now that you know more about The Globe, get ready to compare the theatre in Shakespeare's days with what you know about the theatre today. Prepare individually then exchange orally with your partner and / or with the rest of the class.
If you want the discussion to be lively, do not write full sentences but you can use notes. Use the draft and the suggestions below to organise your ideas.

TIPS
In the following list, choose expressions that will make your viewpoint more personal:

It seems to me that ... • I tend to think that ... • If I'm not mistaken, ... • I'm not sure but I'd say that ... • I may be wrong but I think ... • From what I understood, ...

A Remember the different characteristics of The Globe Theatre in the following fields:

Where and why • Building and Materials • Actors • The Audience • Social Status • Other Forms of Entertainment ...

Make sure you use the appropriate vocabulary by checking Activities 1-4.

B What do you know about the same topics about theatres today?

C When you want to compare or contrast, which of the following tools do you need? Classify them in the table.

more ... than • less ... than • although • in spite of • unlike • as compared to ... • like • as ... as • while

Compare	Contrast

D Now compare and contrast:

Example: The globe was outside London while ...

Your Task

Role-playing a Discussion about the Globe.

A **1. In a group defined by your teacher, get ready to impersonate the character that your teacher assigned.**

Use the role cards below to flesh your character out:
The adjective(s) in parentheses give(s) an idea of your character's personality or mood ;
The job (or religious belief or social status) helps you define the character's viewpoint ;
The other prompts may help you organise your ideas.

Do not write out full sentences but prepare orally and rehearse your role until you are satisfied. Just like an actor or an actress!

To make your character more authentic, you will need the following gap fillers and expressions:
Er ... • I have to say • Well ... • I mean, ... • Of course, ... • You see, ...

B **When your character is ready, you will get together with 4 other characters and role-play a discussion about The Globe and theatre in general.**

When interacting, you will need the following expressions:

It's funny you should say that ... • I can understand but ... • I see your point but ... • It's all very well but ... • It's easy for you to say that ... • No matter what you think, ... • How can you ...? • If I were you ...

TIPS
Don't forget to speak loudly enough to be heard and to make gestures, just like on stage!

Pupil A
I am a rich lady (snobbish)
Never go to The Globe alone
Atmosphere can be shocking
Can understand Puritans but love Shakespeare's plays, especially ...

Pupil B
I am a Puritan (woman or man) (grumpy and austere)
Rarely go to the theatre because ...
Reasons why I don't like The Globe and theatres in general (building, audience, atmosphere, influence, etc.)
If I were the Queen ...
Never met Mr. Shakespeare but ...

Pupil C
I am a male actor (talkative and expressive)
Play Juliet in the play *Romeo and Juliet* (women actresses?)
Reasons why I like The Globe (building, stage, audience's reactions, atmosphere, etc.
Difficult to be an actor at The Globe Theatre = great form of entertainment
Shakespeare = good friend of mine

Pupil D
I am a carpenter (enthusiastic)
Helped build The Globe
Quite proud because ...
Reasons why I love The Globe (building, audience, atmosphere, etc.)
Not very wealthy but I can ...
Met Mr. Shakespeare once, he's ...

Pupil E
I am a 'groundling' (noisy and a little drunk)
The Globe = great fun, cheap entertainment
Standing in the yard = ...
Love the atmosphere
A lot of freedom, can do what I want
If Puritans don't like the theatre ...

Bullying

Activity 1 Defining Bullying

A **Read this definition of bullying with your partner.**

Bullying consists of repeated attacks on the same person by a bully or a group of bullies.

Bullying does not necessarily mean violent, physical assault.

There are three main forms of bullying:

Physical bullying: beating up – hitting – slapping – kicking, etc.

Verbal bullying: gossiping – insulting/calling names – threatening – laughing at/mocking

Psychological and social bullying: ignoring – excluding, etc.

With new technologies (mobiles, the Internet...), new forms of bullying have appeared. They are called **cyberbullying**.

B **Look at the picture on page 29. What forms of bullying do they represent?**

C **1. Then, using the vocabulary above, describe each situation.**

....

2. Bullying exists everywhere. In France it is called: ....

D How can you tell real bullying from jokes or conflicts?

1. Look at the situations and tick the box you agree with.

Situations	Bullying	Conflict	Joking around
One day, someone makes a funny joke about a classmate, everybody laughs, including the classmate.			
X strongly disagrees with Y and they talk about the issue for a long time. They sometimes argue.			
X disagrees with Y about something and calls all his/her friends to have more influence on Y.			
At the beginning of the school year, X said something nasty to Y but it never happened again when they got to know each other.			
During the Physical Education (PE) lesson, every week, X makes fun of Y and sometimes Y cries in the locker room.			

2. Now, compare your answers with your partner. If you disagree, explain your opinion to him/her. All the elements of the situations are useful to explain your point.

Activity 2 Reading Stories of Bullying

Work in pairs. Read these stories and take turns explaining to your partner how you feel about the situation and what you should do about it: go talk to the victim, go talk to the bullies, report the incident to the teachers, ask your parents for advice, etc.
Listen to your partner's explanation and say if you agree.

1. There's a new pupil in the class. She dresses in a way that you find funny. She doesn't wear jeans. Her clothes are more formal than the other pupils. X and Y start pulling at her clothes when they walk past her and call her "Babyface".

2. A pupil doesn't talk much with his schoolmates, he spends break times reading books and never goes out to parties; he prefers to stay on his own. X and Y have stolen his books and torn them up.

3. A pupil likes history and geography and does very well in class. But whenever he puts his hand up, X and Y start booing him and call him a "teacher's pet". After class, they beat him up and tell him it's to teach him how to behave in class.

4. X and Y do not understand the teacher's lesson. So they chat and make noises to get the teacher's attention. They get a special assignment as a punishment. At the end of the class, they stop a classmate and force her to do their assignment for them.

Learn as You Wish

Now that you know more about bullying, to organise your knowledge, choose the method you prefer, A or B. Then explain to your partner what you have understood about the topic of bullying. You may use the following prompts:
I had never heard of ... but I think ... • Did you know that ...? • In my opinion, ... is worse than ... don't you think? • At the beginning, I thought that ... and now, I know that ...

A Fill in the grid below. Some boxes are already filled in to help you. You will be able to fill in more lines later, after doing the other activities.

Examples of bullying	Types of bullying	Suggestions to solve the problem
beating up, hitting, slapping, kicking	physical bullying	
gossiping, insulting, calling names, threatening, laughing at, mocking		
ignoring, excluding		

MP3 **B** **Review all the vocabulary your have learned about bullying thanks to the following cloud. Do not forget to listen to the words as well. Then, using the words, make sentences to explain what bullying is, to give examples, to react, etc.**

Example: *Ignoring and excluding classmates or making fun of them is psychological bullying and it may be worse than violent physical assault sometimes.*

repeated attacks **bullies** violent

physical assault **beat up** **hit** **slap** kick

verbal bullying **gossip** **insult**

call names **threaten** laugh at **mocking**

psychological bullying **social bullying** ignore exclude

mobile phone the Internet **cyberbullying** argue advice

help make fun of **quarrel** nasty message **anonymous**

lonely worthless **confront** relieved **cowards** cyberbully

rude Facebook account **abusive** photoshopped images

comments **posts** volunteer

....

....

....

....

....

....

....

Activity 3 Comparing Stories

A Read the short texts then answer the questions.

Georgia, a young girl from Kent, England, experienced cyberbullying when she was thirteen years old. It all started after she and one of her friends had a quarrel. She started receiving nasty messages on a social networks and on her phone for a few weeks. Anonymous people would insult her and create stories about her. She felt lonely, had no friends and slowly began to believe everything the bullies said. She thought she was worthless. But fortunately, while cleaning her room, her mum found poems and drawings that made her understand everything. So her mum and dad confronted Georgia and she told them everything. She felt relieved afterwards. Her parents deleted her social accounts on the net and changed her phone number. She has since realised that bullies are just cowards sitting behind a screen.

Khushal, 17, from London, was cyberbullied through Facebook. Someone created an account in his name and put horrible photoshopped images of him and used it to send rude and abusive comments. Worse, almost his entire year group of pupils had added him as a friend, and were seeing all the posts. At first Khushal couldn't understand why people were behaving strangely towards him. Eventually, he discovered the fake account. A friend accompanied him to talk to teachers about it. The school asked Facebook to delete the account, which they eventually did. Thanks to a lot of support from friends, teachers and his parents, Khushal has now become a volunteer to help other victims of cyberbullying.

1. Write down all the elements describing how Georgia felt about the situation.

....

....

2. Who helped Georgia and Khushal?

Georgia: ....

Khushal: ....

3. Georgia's story and Khushal's story have 2 elements in common. What are they?

....

....

4. What was Khushal's reaction after the incident?

....

....

B Add these two new situations to the grid on page 30 or add new vocabulary on page 31.

C In the following list of adjectives, pick the ones that you think describe best the way victims of bullying feel. Be ready to explain your choice.

anxious • confident • depressed • energetic • extroverted • humiliated • indifferent • introverted • open • optimistic • pessimistic • revengeful • shy

Activity 4 Listening to an Interview

A Anticipation.

1. Before you listen to Matt May's interview, review all the vocabulary you have learned about bullying by looking at A or B on pages 30-31.

2. Matt works for an organisation called Beatbullying. What do you think the organisation does to fight bullying?

☐ punishing bullies ☐ designing websites ☐ giving interviews on TV ☐ writing articles

☐ training people to help and support victims

B Understanding the interview.

1. a. First listening. As you listen, circle the words you hear.

repeated attacks **bullies** violent physical assault **beat up** **hit** **slap** kick
verbal bullying **gossip** **insult** call names **threaten** laugh at
mocking psychological bullying **social bullying** ignore exclude
mobile phone the Internet **cyberbullying** upset advice **help**
make fun of **quarrel** nasty message **anonymous** **lonely**
worthless **confront** relieved **cowards** cyberbully **rude**
Facebook account **abusive** photoshopped images **comments**
posts volunteer intimidate

b. What form of bullying is mentioned in the interview? ....

c. Look at the words you circled and give a short definition of this form of bullying.

....

2. Second listening. Answer the following by ticking the right elements.

a. In the UK ☐ 1 in 10 ☐ 1 in 3 ☐ 1 in 5 young people have experienced this form of bullying.

b. The problem is ☐ increasing ☐ diminishing ☐ remaining stable.

c. What are the best ways to avoid the problem?

☐ never send text messages ☐ do not forward text messages ☐ do not join social media

☐ talk to your friends only ☐ talk to adults about it ☐ stop using your computer

☐ look for online support

3. Third listening. Go back to B1. Listen again. Do you hear words you didn't hear the first time?

C Now use A and B to sum up what you understood about Matt's interview.

Your Task

Making a Poster and Leaflet for Anti-Bullying Week

A **All the pupils at your school are invited to contribute for the anti-bullying week. You are going to work in groups and each group has to do 2 things:**

1. Produce a poster with: a clear definition (in your own words) of what bullying is, visual elements with captions and a catchy slogan to fight bullying.

2. Design a leaflet or a brochure. You can choose from the following elements: the slogan(s) of your campaign; drawings, collages, logos, photographs with captions; a short testimony of someone who has been bullied or a short interview; advice and solutions to fight bullying; a list of dos and don'ts.

If you would like help finding ideas, we have selected some websites to help you.

@ CONNECT TO: collegien.nathan.fr/speak3

You can make your plan for your poster here.
For the leaflet, there are lots of different formats: 2, 4 or 6 pages, different sizes. With your group, choose the format you think works best for the information
you want to transmit.

B **As you work, think about the following evaluation criteria:**

1. Evaluation for Group Work

- Contributes regularly to group discussions
- Speaks English only
- Makes constructive suggestions
- Demonstrates a cooperative attitude
- Contributes to the success of the project

2. Evaluation of poster/leaflet

- Visual quality
- Originality, creativity
- Precision of explanations
- Useful information
- Relevant advice

British Food

Activity 1 Food and Stereotypes

A **To find out about common stereotypes about French or British food, fill in the following bubbles with the right words: *the French* or *the British*.**

……………………

eat frog legs every Sunday.

……………………
put garlic in every dish they cook.

……………………
do not know how to make good cheese.

……………………

eat disgusting things such as snails.

……………………
eat disgusting things such as meat with mint sauce.

……………………
eat boiled meat.

B **Discuss your answers with your partner, then tell her/him what you think of the stereotypes about French food.**

So, in your opinion, what is the definition of a cultural stereotype?

- ☐ Something that is always true and describes a country and its people very well.
- ☐ Something that is never true and is invented to hurt people's feelings.
- ☐ Something that is (or was) true sometimes but is generalised to a whole country.

Learn as You Wish

Some British dishes are very popular in France. Read about a dish. Choose what you prefer, A or B, a story or a recipe.

A

History of the Sandwich

It got its name from an 18th-century English aristocrat, John Montague, Earl of Sandwich, who liked eating meat between two slices of bread. Supposedly, he particularly liked this meal because he could eat it and continue to play cards without getting his hands dirty. Although he did not invent the sandwich, his name is forever associated with this easy-to-carry food.

B

Apple Crumble

1. Peel, core and chop 900g of apples. Squeeze lemon juice over the apples.

2. Layer the apples and 175g of sugar in a large pie dish.

3. Mix 600g of flour and 400g of butter until it resembles breadcrumbs, and sprinkle the mixture over the fruit.

4. Bake for 45 minutes.

Activity 2 Interviews about Food

Interview four pupils in the class and take notes. Don't forget to answer the questions yourself.

Questions	Me	Name:	Name:	Name:	Name: ....
1. British specialities you are willing to try.					
2. British specialities you have actually tasted.					
3. Did you like them?					
4. French specialities that could seem strange to foreigners.					

MP3

TIPS

Prepare for listening to the other groups. Listen and practise saying useful phrases.

Can you speak louder? • I didn't hear the result for question x, could you repeat it, please? • Could you write … on the board? • Would you mind explaining … ? • I didn't understand … • Can you speak a little more slowly, please? • I didn't have time to write …, can you repeat, please?

Learn as You Wish

Interpreting a survey. While the different groups report to the class, take notes below. Then choose the method you prefer for interpreting, A or B.

Questions	Results Group 1	Results Group 2	Results Group 3	Results Group 4	Results Group 5
1. British specialities you are willing to try.					
2. British specialities you have actually tasted.					
3. Did you like them?					
4. French specialities that could seem strange to foreigners					

A The numbers. You can use this outline:

.... are willing to try .... but .... have never tasted British specialities.

.... who have already tasted British specialities like them but .... didn't.

.... mentioned .... as a French speciality that could seem strange to foreigners.

B Your opinion. You can use this outline:

I find it surprising that ....

I thought that more pupils would have ....

I didn't think that so many / so few pupils would have ....

Activity 3 Fish and Chips

MP3 **A** **Listen to Part 1. Complete the sentences with the suggested words.**

1. The first fish and chip shop... (1860 • fish market • London)

....

2. The biggest fish and chip shop (North of England • 250 customers • a million customers)

....

....

MP3 **B** **Listen to Part 2. The recipe for fish and chips.**

1. Tick what you hear.

a. The most common fish is ☐ salmon ☐ haddock ☐ cod.

b. The fish is dipped in ☐ batter ☐ butter.

c. The chips are ☐ thin ☐ thick.

2. Listen, then put the pictures in the order of the recipe and write a caption for each image.

....

....

....

Activity 4 British Food Webquest

1. @ CONNECT TO: collegien.nathan.fr/speak3 **Click on the "Food and drink" section. Read about meals and food, and fill in this table about British food.**

Meals	Traditionally	Today
Breakfast		

2. Explore the site and find answers to the questions.

a. A love-it-or-hate-it sauce:

Name? ....

Ingredients? ....

Aspect? ....

b. Sunday roast: what does it consist of? ....

....

c. Difference between afternoon tea and high tea? ....

....

Your Task

Create a Quiz about British Food

Work in groups of four.

Prepare a quiz about British food composed of eight questions with multiple-choice or right/wrong answers. Then test another group.

....

....

....

....

....

....

....

The Windrush Generation

Activity 1 Commenting on Pictures

A Look at the following pictures and map. Then answer the question on page 41.

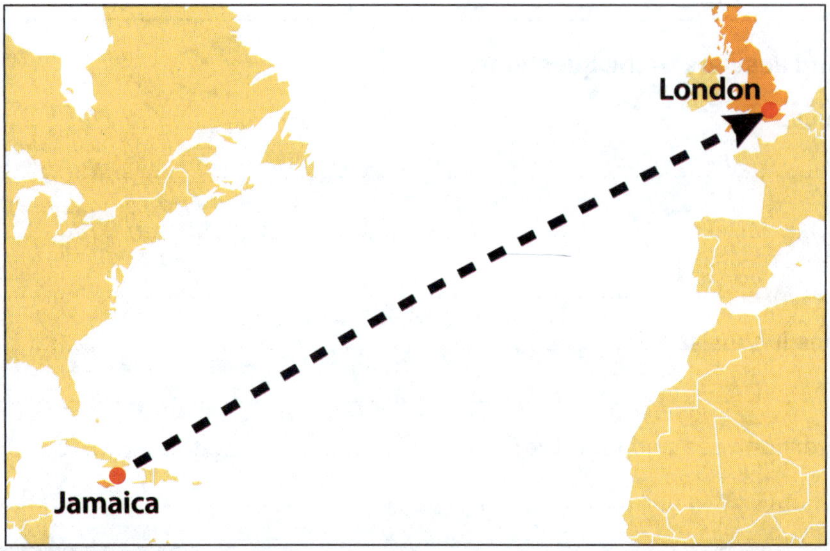

1. The context?

a. Approximate date according to the photos? ....

b. Subject illustrated by the pictures? ....

2. Imagine who these people are.

a. Where from? ....

b. Imagine why they left. ....

c. Where to? ....

d. Hopes and desires? ....

e. Imagine how they feel and explain why.

sad • homesick • happy • excited • worried • exhausted (= very tired) • ...

....

....

....

3. Get ready to use your notes to comment on the pictures orally.

TIPS
For help with oral presentations, see Learn As You Wish, page 44.

B @ CONNECT TO: collegien.nathan.fr/speak3

1. Read the web page and check your hypotheses from A.

2. Find the following elements to complete your oral presentation:

a. Exact date of the arrival? ....

b. Reasons why the British authorities encouraged people from the West Indies to come?

....

c. Number of migrants? ....

d. What did the migrants expect to find in Britain? What attracted them there?

....

e. The majority of them...

☐ *returned to the West Indies after a few years.* ☐ *settled and stayed in Britain permanently.*

f. Impact on British society?

....

3. Comment on the pictures orally.

Activity 2 Reading Migrants' Testimonies

Read the testimony your teacher assigned to your group.

Group A

A @ CONNECT TO: collegien.nathan.fr/speak3

Read Clinton Edward's testimony.
Complete the following spidergram about Clinton Edwards.

In Britain after the destruction of World War 2, there was lots of work for the immigrants.

Clinton Edwards

- World War 2?
- Reasons for leaving Jamaica?
- Personal details?
- Life in England?
- Job(s)? – Family?
- Jamaica/England now?

B **To help you better understand the text, match the following words from the text to their definitions.**

1. RAF •	• **a.** Money you pay for a bus, boat, train or plane ticket.
2. fare •	• **b.** Someone who is not in the military.
3. I got demobbed •	• **c.** Painful, hurtful, that brings pain and discomfort.
4. civilian •	• **d.** Royal Air Force.
5. welder •	• **e.** Colleagues.
6. wheelbarrow •	• **f.** Family, people you are related to.
7. shovel •	• **g.** I returned to civilian life.
8. sore •	• **h.** A tool you use to dig holes.
9. work mates •	• **i.** A worker who joins pieces of metal by heating them.
10. relatives •	• **j.** A cart used to carry heavy things in gardens or construction sites.

C **Work with people from Group B and exchange information.**

1. Get ready to use the spidergram to present Clinton orally.

2. Take notes about the other Windrush passenger.

TIPS
For help with oral presentations, see Learn As You Wish, page 44.

Read Vince Reid's testimony.

Group B

A @ CONNECT TO: collegien.nathan.fr/speak3

The following statements are all RIGHT. Quote elements from the text to prove it.

1. Vince Reid didn't decide to leave Jamaica. He had no choice!

....

2. He was a boy when he arrived in England.

....

3. He suffered from racism and felt quite lonely at school.

....

4. Things got better when he joined the military.

....

5. He prefers life in England, even if there are problems.

....

B **Get ready to present Vince Reid orally.**
Use elements from question A and from the text to reformulate things. Write some sentences of your own.

1. Explain when and why he left Jamaica. ....

....

2. Talk about his experience of racism when he was at school. ....

....

3. Say how he felt about it. ....

....

4. Explain what he did in life. ....

....

5. Say if he wants to go back to Jamaica. ....

....

6. Express what he thinks of England. ....

....

C **Work with people from Group A and exchange information.**

1. Present Vince orally.

2. Take notes about the other Windrush passenger.

TIPS
For help with oral presentations, see Learn As You Wish, page 44.

Learn as You Wish

Remember that when you speak, even in your native language, you often hesitate, start something and then change your mind. In English, it is perfectly normal to do it as well. In that case, use gap fillers such as: *well – you know – I mean – let me explain – er...*

To practise, choose the method you prefer, A or B.

A Record yourself talking about a subject you are comfortable with, in French. Listen to see where you hesitate and gap fill. Try to do the same in English!

MP3 **B** Listen to the recording and note the gap fillers. Try to do the same!

Activity 3 Writing Another Testimony

A Create your character.

1. Name? ....

2. Age in 1948? ....

3. Reason(s) for coming to England?

economic • curiosity • no future in Jamaica • love • not your decision • job • family already in England

4. First impressions when you arrived?

....

....

5. Problems you faced? Difficulties you had?

....

....

6. How you felt about it?

....

....

7. Your opinion about England 50 years after? Would you go back to Jamaica? Why?

....

....

B Write the testimony of the character you created.

Don't forget that, just like Clinton and Vince, you are going to mention past events, so you need to use the simple past!

Activity 4 Reading about the Impact on British Culture and Society

A Anticipate. Do you know anything about the Caribbean influence on British society? Look at the photos. Can you guess?

a. Music? ....

b. Special event(s)? Festival? ....

c. Customs? ....

B Read the following text about West Indian immigration in Britain. Check your ideas and answer the questions.

The arrival of *The Windrush* at Tilbury Docks in 1948 opened the way to more immigration from the Caribbean. In the 1950s more and more people from the Caribbean arrived in London and settled there. With the growing number of immigrants, some English people started protesting because they had the impression that migrants took their jobs and houses. There were racist attacks and incidents and there were even race riots (= explosions of street violence) in 1958.

In response to that, Caribbean people decided to develop a Caribbean pride and share their cultural heritage with the British community. For example, reggae music started to become popular. The Notting Hill Carnival, in London every August, attracted more and more British non-Caribbean people with its colourful costumes, dances, parades and its drum and steel bands. Other Caribbean communities in big cities such as Cardiff, Birmingham... soon followed the trend and organised their own carnivals. Today, the Notting Hill Carnival is Europe's biggest street festival.

1. In the text, underline:

a. problems faced by the Caribbean community in blue.

b. elements of their culture they wanted to share in red.

2. Complete the following sentences recapping the text.

a. In the 1950s, there were housing and employment problems. As a result/Consequently ....

....

b. Because of racism, people from the Caribbean decided to ....

....

c. They wanted to share their culture in order (not) to ....

....

Your Task

Writing a Letter to Support "Windrush Day"

Patrick Vernon, a documentary film maker of Caribbean descent, wants British authorities to create a "Windrush Day" to celebrate British people of Caribbean descent. He often publishes articles and speaks in the media in favour of this idea.
You are the grandchild of one of the West Indians who arrived on board the Windrush in 1948. You have decided to write to your local MP (Member of Parliament) to support Patrick Vernon's idea.

In your letter, you must:

a. introduce yourself;

b. explain why you are writing;

c. talk about your grandfather/mother (*why he/she came, what he/she did, problems he/she faced...*);

d. insist on the impact of Caribbean influence on British culture.

Dear Member of Parliament,

Yours respectfully.

Jeff Koons

Activity 1 Pop Art

The term Pop Art was invented in 1955 to describe a new form of art characterised by the link between consumer society and popular culture. In the 1960s, it became the major art style.

Pop Art uses bright colours and everyday images. Advertisements, product packaging, and comic strips were sources of inspiration for Pop artists.

The most famous Pop artists are probably Andy Warhol and Roy Lichtenstein. Their message was that art could be made from very simple materials. It was a way for them to rebel against the art forms of the past.

Today, artists like Jeff Koons and David Hockney continue the pop art style.

Roy Lichtenstein *Vicki! I--I Thought I Heard Your Voice!* 1964

One of Andy Warhol's series of prints of Campbell's soup cans.

Write what you know about Pop Art in this mind map. Then read the text and look at the images on page 48 and add to it. You can add more infomation to the mind map as you do the different activities.

Pop Art

- Objectives?
- Subjects?
- Colours, Aspect and Shapes?
- Artists?
- When?

Activity 2 Listening to a conversation

MP3 A **1. Listen to Part 1 and complete:**

a. Type of works in the room? ....

b. Title of the piece? ....

c. Artist? ....

d. Nationality? ....

e. City of residence? ....

f. It is:
- ☐ a basketball suspended in a gas box.
- ☐ a basketball suspended in a glass box.
- ☐ a basket roll suspended in a glass box.

2. a. There ☐ is something ☐ isn't anything special about the object.

b. Pick out elements to prove your point. ....

3. a. Complete the sentence with the right words:

I .... work out how it's suspended. There .... a cable.

It .... move. I .... think there's water.

b. Now practise saying the complete sentence with the correct intonation.

4. What do they think of the sculpture?

a. Person 1: ....

b. Person 2: ....

Learn as You Wish

How to translate visual language into words. Part 1

Classify the following elements. Choose the organisation you prefer, A or B.

colour • shape • techniques used • surfaces and textures • size • composition • date of creation • place of creation • artist's biography • link with other art works or artists • what it is about • portrait • landscape • abstract • title • realistic • message • materials • what feeling • what atmosphere • harmony • mood • artist's intention • effect created

A

Description	Formal analysis	Interpretation	Judgement

B

Art

What do I see?

How is the artwork made and organised?

What does the artwork mean?

What do I think about the artwork?

Group A Do Activity 2B on this page. **Group B** Your Activity 2B is on page 77.

Group A

MP3

B Listen to Part 2.

1. The sculpture

a. Title? ....

b. What does it look like? ....

c. Size? ....

d. Material? ....

e. Colour and aspect? ....

f. Other details? ....

2. What do we understand about the second person in the end?

....

3. Try to draw the sculpture in the box on the right.

Learn as You Wish

How to translate visual language into words. Part 2

Use the 4 categories you chose in Part 1 to classify the questions that you must ask yourself when looking at an artwork:

How is it organised?

What is the use of colours?

What shapes are used?

Does it remind me of another art piece?

What did the artist want to tell me?

Is it realistic or symbolic?

Does it make me feel in a particular way?

What is my first reaction?

Do I like it? Why or why not?

What do I know about the artist?

Does it illustrate a specific theme?

Activity 3 Your Opinion About Art

Get ready to discuss the artworks on this page and page 48 with your partner.

a. Select one of the works of art. Get ready to describe it (shapes, colours, size, material...) to your partner. Then, swap roles.

b. Get ready to explain why you selected this work of art. Develop what you like about it, how it makes you feel, what it suggests, etc. and discuss this with your partner.

Words

Personally, I think... • For me... • In my opinion... • As far as I'm concerned... • I agree with... • I don't agree with...

Jeff Koons, *Michael Jackson and Bubbles*, 1988

John Singer Sargent, *Lady Agnew of Lucknow*, 1892-93

Your Task

Role-playing a Debate

Get ready to debate Jeff Koons' work.

Pupil A
You love Jeff Koons' art. You think it's fantastic. You disagree with people who don't like it. For you, it is art because it shows ordinary objects in extraordinary contexts.

Pupil B
You hate Jeff Koons' art. You think it is just a way to make money with ordinary objects. You don't understand why it's called art.

Pupil C
You don't really like Jeff Koons' art. But you agree with pupil A and you think that it actually is art.

Pupil D
You like Jeff Koons' work, you think it's fun. But compared to other artists, it isn't art. You believe he sells a product, not art.

Building Europe

Activity 1 Getting to Know the European Union

@ CONNECT TO: collegien.nathan.fr/speak3

A **Log on to the website, choose English and play the game.**

B **Place the words in the correct box on the map.**

border • capital • country • inhabitant • region • flag • anthem

C 1. Get to know the E.U. Read the text.

The 50 stars on the American flag represent the 50 states of the U.S.A. But the 12 stars on the European flag cannot represent the European states since the E.U. is made up of 28 European countries. (The total population is about 503 million). Two western European countries are not in the Union (one is in Northern Europe and the other has been a neutral country for centuries).

2. Name the two countries that are not in the E.U. or trying to join it. Need some help?
@ CONNECT TO: collegien.nathan.fr/speak3
Click on "Read an online book to learn and discover Europe." Go to page 37. (The book may open in your internet browser or download as a pdf.)

In colour, the E.U. countries. The ones in grey are candidates to join the E.U.

Activity 2 Building the Union

A **1. Look at the following nouns and dates and tell your partner what you know about them.**

1939-1945 • The U.K. • the E.E.C. • the E.U. • 1951–1957

2. Take notes of what you know and what your partner tells you in the "What we know" column. Use a pencil so you can erase easily.

3. With your partner, fill in the "What we want to know" column. Jot down words, do not write long sentences.

EUROPE	What we know	What we Want to know	What we learned	What we still want to know
Important dates				
Countries				
Important people				
Different names				
Original members				
Symbols				

B Read the text and use the reading strategy you prefer from the Learn As You Wish box.

Together for Peace

Jean Monnet

From 1914 to 1945, Europe fought two world wars, and millions of Europeans died. After World War Two, Jean Monnet, a French economist and negotiator, wanted to encourage the different countries to cooperate, instead of fighting. Politicians like Winston Churchill in the U.K., Robert Schuman in France, Konrad Adenauer in West Germany and Altiero Spinelli in Italy, were also convinced of the necessity of creating a pacified and strong European union. Monnet suggested a union of the coal and steel industries (the European Coal and Steel Community or E.C.S.C.) because those are industries that are important for making weapons and bombs. It was created in 1951, and on 25th March 1957, its six members (Belgium, France, Germany, Italy, Luxembourg and the Netherlands) created the European Economic Community.

The E.E.C. adopted a blue flag with a circle of gold stars. The 12 stars symbolise the peace and harmony (and also prosperity) that Europeans wished for.

Together for Understanding

Many pro-Europeans thought that if ordinary Europeans had more opportunities to meet people from other countries, they would understand them better and that would encourage peace. From the beginning, the E.E.C. wanted to make it easier for products to move between countries, but also for people. As the E.E.C. grew (and changed its name to the E.U.), this became easier and easier.

Notes

....

....

....

....

Learn as You Wish

Reading Strategies

You don't have to do the activities in chronological order and you don't have to do all of them. Don't forget to write down what you find out under "What we learned" in the appropriate boxes. Use a pencil. Choose the method you prefer, A, B or C.

A 1. Scan the text and look for information about people, dates and the nouns in Activity 2. A.1. Highlight them.

2. Without looking at the text again, use the table on page 55 above to sum up what you have understood. Be ready to report to the class.

B 1. Match the following topics mentioned in the text to the appropriate dates.

Creation of the E.E.C. •	• 1914 to 1945
Two world wars in Europe •	• 1951
Creation of the European Coal and Steel Community •	• 1957

2. Match the people and their status. Be careful, not all the statuses will be used and several people can have the same.

Jean Monnet •	• Industrialist
Winston Churchill •	• Fighter
Robert Schuman •	• Negotiator
Konrad Adenauer •	• Government member
Altiero Spinelli •	

3. Match the people and their objectives. Be careful, not all the objectives will be used, one person can have two objectives and several people can have the same.

Jean Monnet •	
Winston Churchill •	• wanted to promote peace in Europe
Robert Schuman •	• wanted cooperation in Europe
Konrad Adenauer •	• wanted more understanding between countries
Altiero Spinelli •	• wanted Europe to be powerful
Pro-Europeans •	

4. Without looking at the text again, use the table on page 55 to sum up what you have understood. Be ready to report to the class.

C 1. Scan the text and find important facts about Europe. Highlight them.

2. Scan the text and look for verbs or words that evoke opinions as opposed to facts. Highlight them then explain what the different people's opinions about Europe are. You may use the following prompts.

.... believed that ....

In ....'s opinion, Europe ....

The European Union is / was considered as .... by ....

The European Union is / was believed to be ....

3. Without looking at the text again, use the table page 55 to sum up what you have understood. Be ready to report to the class.

Activity 3 From War to Peace

Look at the timeline of Europe in the 20th century. Choose the correct events from the box for each date or period.

Civil War in Spain • the fall of the Berlin Wall • Peace but an arms race • Peace but two blocs: the West and the East (Communist) • World War I • World War II

1919-1939 — *1945-1989* — *1989*

1914-1918 — *1936-1939* — *1939-1945*

Activity 4 Playing a European Quiz

A **Listen and play the quiz in teams.**

B **Listen again and put the words in the column corresponding to the pronunciation of <i>. Some words, with two <i> sounds, go in both columns.**

win • invited • five • trip • symbolise • unity • solidarity • splendid • city • inhabitants • give • figure

ɪ	aɪ

Activity 5 The Main Treaties of the E.U.

A **Read the text.**

The **Treaty of Rome** established the E.E.C. (European Economic Community) in 1957. It was at the origin of the European common market, which became the European Union. For example, if a German family visits France, they can buy anything they want. They don't have to pay duty.
The 1985 **Schengen Agreement** created a zone abolishing border controls between member countries. To make life easier for travellers, most E.E.C. countries had got rid of passport checks at the borders between them. A person living in one member country was free to go and live and find work in any other member country.
The Maastricht Treaty prepared for monetary union and the euro. It was signed in 1992. Now in many E.U. countries (but not the UK, nor Denmark), people pay in euros.

Words
duty: special taxes on imports

B **1. Read the statements and decide what Heidi and Helmut, Juan and Sarah *have to / don't have to / can / cannot* do in the E.U.**

change currency • show passport at the border • get a work permit • pay with his/her/their national currency • pay at Customs • pass the border without a problem

a. Heidi and Helmut from Frankfurt are visiting France during the holidays.

....

b. Juan is a truck driver transporting fruit from Spain to the Netherlands.

....

c. Sarah, a British teacher, is applying for a job in France.

....

2. What about their parents, before the treaties?

Use: had to • used to • were not able to

a. ....

b. ....

c. ....

Your Task

Presenting Europe

Your school is twinned with a school in Australia. With your group, prepare a PowerPoint or Photorécit presentation about Europe and the way we live here that you will send to the class.

Explain what the E.U is (number of countries, currency, free circulation...).

@ CONNECT TO: collegien.nathan.fr/speak3

Browse through the book you downloaded (p. 1-21) or explore the map for extra information. You will find links to make your presentation online, too.

If you wish, you can use these elements to plan your presentation.

1. Review what you have learned. Decide the elements you are going to need. Locate the resources on the Internet and import them:

Title for the presentation / headlines for each slide / archive pictures / photos / portraits / maps / drawings / captions / mind maps / a quiz on the last slide to get the viewers involved / sound: excerpts of famous speeches, the European anthem...

2. Point of view: what do you want to do with your presentation, besides informing your penfriends?

Convincing, provoking, questioning, defending?...

3. Use boxes like the one below to plan what each slide is supposed to show.

On the right, write the script you will record. Use a pencil as you might change your mind several times! Rehearse until you are satisfied with the result.

Remember that the script should not repeat what the slide shows. Decide what information is best on the slide, and what is best said.

Slide 1

Script

....

....

....

....

....

....

....

....

War Horse

Activity 1 Watching a Trailer

@ CONNECT TO: collegien.nathan.fr/speak3

Watch the trailer with the SOUND OFF, and take some notes.

1. Title?

....

2. Subject?

....

3. Characters?

....

4. Theatre technique?

....

5. What will happen next?

....

Activity 2 World War One

MP3 **Write the words in the corresponding places on the picture of a World War One battlefield:**

Allied trenches • German-Austrian trenches • No Man's Land • barbed wire

War Child to War Horse

Michael Morpurgo was born in 1943 and grew up in London. It was during World War Two, a period he has often written about. Morpurgo was first a military officer, then a teacher. In 1976, he and his wife Clare created a charity called Farms for City Children. They have three farms where children from the city go to spend a week discovering farming life.
But Morpurgo is best known as one of Britain's most popular authors for children and teenagers. He has written more than 130 books on varied subjects, although many are about war, animals or animals and war. His books include *Kensuke's Kingdom, Private Peaceful, The Butterfly Lion, The Eagle in the Snow* and of course, *War Horse*. It was adapted as a very popular play by the British National Theatre and as film by Steven Spielberg.

Activity 3 Listening to an Interview

A You are going to listen to Helena Stride of the Imperial War Museum in London summarising the story of *War Horse* by Michael Morpurgo. Organise what you already know about the story and write the answers you already know to the questions below.

....

....

B 1. Listen to Part 1 and complete your answers from what you hear.

a. Horse's name: ....

b. Boy's name: ....

c. Farm in: ....

d. Horse sent to: ....

e. Horse's occupation there: either .... or ....

2. What do we learn about the boy when the horse is sold?

a. He's ☐ depressed ☐ upset ☐ revolted.

b. He ☐ asks his parents to help him find the horse ☐ goes to the police ☐ joins the Army to find the horse.

C Listen to Part 2.

1. Number the events in chronological order.
The horse is...

☐ **a.** found by French civilians.

☐ **b.** used as a transport horse.

☐ **c.** captured by the German army.

☐ **d.** reunited with Albert.

2. Helena uses the word "eventually" on two occasions. Does it mean:

☐ **a.** possibly? ☐ **b.** finally?

D Complete:

1. Using a horse as the main protagonist was an opportunity to look at the war ☐ from the German side ☐ from both sides ☐ from the British side.

2. The horse is used as a kind of ☐ neutral ☐ positive ☐ humanlike element between the two.

Activity 4

A **There are five episodes to the story. Read the episode that the teacher has assigned to you and fill your part in the table in Your Task (next page).**

B **Now, using your notes and the rest of the worksheet, decide where in the narrative your episode probably is from (1 beginning, to 5 end). Highlight, in your episode, the elements that were mentioned in Activities 1, 2 and 3 and helped you make your decision.**

My episode is probably 1, 2, ... because ....

....

Learn as You Wish

Style and Meaning

An author uses different elements such as narrative style or figures of speech (images), to make the story interesting. Choose what you want to explore, A or B.

A Narrative Style

When the narrator tells a story by using "I", it is a first-person narrative: the story is narrated from his/her point of view.

1. Read your episode again and say who "I" is.

....

2. Is it a first-person narrative? Why or why not?

....

3. Choose in the following list the elements which correspond best to the narration.

The narration is:

☐ objective. ☐ subjective. ☐ We only learn about events.

☐ We learn about events and about the narrator's feelings. ☐ We know what the narrator thinks. ☐ We don't know what the narrator thinks.

4. Look at the following words and say what makes *War Horse* original.

First-person narrative • think • feelings

....

....

B Figures of Speech

First match the figures of speech to the appropriate definitions. Then choose the stylistic device that is used in *War Horse*.

Personification •	• A comparison between two unlike things that have something in common.
Metaphor •	• A use of words to express the opposite of their literal meaning.
Understatement •	• A figure of speech in which a non-human thing has human qualities or abilities.
Irony •	• A figure of speech in which a situation seems less important than it is.

Your Task

Telling Your Episode

A **Be ready to tell your episode back in class <u>in your own words</u>.**

Keep your presentation short and lively. Rehearse until you are satisfied with your presentation. You can record yourself or ask a partner to make a video of your presentation so you can work on body language and gestures. You can use the following prompts if you need to:

In the episode I had to read • The action was set in • The passage describes / explains / presents / shows / tells the story of • Joey, the main protagonist, tells us about • He meets • He works for • He has to • His problem in this episode is

TIPS

Don't forget to link the parts:
at the beginning • then • after that • later on • eventually = finally • in the end

B **While listening to other people report to the class, take notes of what they say so you can decide where their episode is. In the last two lines, you will assess the presentations and give advice to the reporters.**

Questions	My episode	Reporter's name	Reporter's name	Reporter's name	Reporter's name
Where: country, region, particular place if specified.					
Who: people, nationality, name, age.					
What: what Joey does, what happens to him.					
Feelings: how Joey and other characters feel in this episode.					
Assessment of the presentation: voice, body language and eye contact, fluency, comprehensibility, interest, etc.					
Suggestions for the reporter.					

New York, New York

Activity 1 Reading about New York's Five Boroughs

A **Work in pairs.**

Pupil A **Do Activity 2A on pp. 66-67.** **Pupil B** **Your Activity 2A is on pp. 78-79.**

Pupil A
Read about Manhattan, The Bronx and Queens.

Unique New York

New York is a cultural melting pot of people of different races, ethnicities, religions, points of view and professions. With great street food, museums, art galleries and Broadway theatres, restaurants, shopping and parks, New York has something for everyone.

Central Park

Manhattan

While Manhattanites tend to see their island as the centre of the universe, you have to admit that they have some good reasons. It is the most-visited, best-known and smallest of the five boroughs, being home to NYC landmarks like Times Square, Wall Street, Broadway, and Central Park. Although this is where you can see native celebs from Robert de Niro and Woody Allen to Lady Gaga... it retains a neighbourly feeling in many areas.

"The City" – as any self-respecting New Yorker calls it – is made up of five boroughs, which were designated in 1898: Manhattan, Brooklyn, Queens, The Bronx, and Staten Island.

Queens

Queens, the largest of the boroughs, was supposedly named for Portuguese Queen Catherine of Braganza, who married King Charles II of Britain in 1662.
Queens is a multi-ethnic borough with South and Central American, Greek, Central European, Indian and other communities.
Jackson Heights was the first "garden city" community built in the U.S., in the 1910s-20s.
It is still a pleasant area with tree-lined streets of brownstone apartment buildings.
Jazz was important to the area in the 1940s.
Musicians like Louis Armstrong and Ella Fitzgerald escaped Segregation in the racially mixed communities of Queens, and more recent artists like LL Cool J, Nas and Run-D.M.C. all found their start in this borough.

"Brownstone" apartment buildings

The Bronx

North of Manhattan, the Bronx has a tough reputation for violence and crime. Yet locals are quick to defend their borough. African-Americans, Africans, Jamaicans, Italians and Latinos make up a lively multi-ethnic community, where music holds pride of place. Movies like Spike Lee's *Summer of Sam*, and Walter Hill's *The Warriors* have helped shape the Bronx's gritty urban image. But the Bronx has a kinder, gentler side too: Yankee Stadium, home to the city's 27-time World Champion baseball team, is here, and parents love to take their children to the Bronx Zoo, where rare endangered species can be seen.

The Bronx is a great place to find street art.

B **Locate the three boroughs you read about on the map and ask your partner questions to find the other two.**

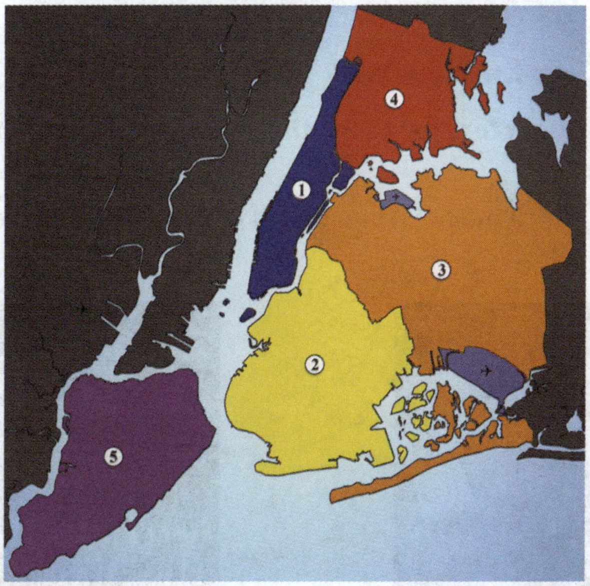

1. ....
2. ....
3. ....
4. ....
5. ....

MP3 **C** **Listen to check your answers and practise the pronunciation of the place names.**

D **Ask your partner questions to complete the information on the population chart. How many...? How big...?**

The five boroughs' area and population:

Brooklyn	183 km^2	
The Bronx	100 km^2	
Manhattan		1,629,000
Queens	283 km^2	
Staten Island		470,000

Activity 2 Comparing Boroughs

Compare the five boroughs using the following prompts.

Characteristics: populated • famous • small • large • known • attractive • quiet • busy • high density
Comparative: more • less • *adj*+er
Superlative: most • least • *adj*+est

Learn as You Wish

Getting a Feel for New York City

New York City has inspired film directors for a long time. Choose the film-linked activity you prefer, A or B.

A Look at the film posters and say which movie(s) you would like to see. Be ready to explain why.

Directed by
Martin Scorsese, 1976

Directed by
Spike Lee, 1989

Directed by
Martin Scorsese, 2002

B Film locations. Check the following film locations on the Internet (type the names in your browser) and say which film(s) best represent(s) New York City in your opinion. Be ready to explain your choice.

1. *Manhattan*: Riverview Terrace Sutton Square, Empire Diner, Elaine's Restaurant, Guggenheim Museum, Hayden Planetarium.
2. *Ghostbusters*: North Moore Street Firehouse, New York Public Library, Columbia University, 55 Central Park West.
3. *Taxi Driver*: Times Square, Hilton Theater, Columbus Circle.
4. *The Devil Wears Prada*: McGraw-Hill Building, Bubby's Hudson Street, Smith and Wollensky.

Activity 3 Manhattan's Monuments and Landmarks

Now let's concentrate on Manhattan. Match the definitions and the names of the places. Then write the number on the corresponding spot on the map.

The Empire State Building

The Guggenheim Museum

"Lady Liberty"

Places	Definitions
1. Museum Mile (Fifth Ave., 68th to 103rd Streets) •	• **a.** This monument was a present from France to the U.S.A. to celebrate American independence.
2. Empire State Building (Fifth Avenue/33rd to 35th Streets) •	• **b.** A building where all nations meet to work towards world peace and human rights.
3. Ground Zero (southern tip, just north-west of Wall Street) •	• **c.** The financial district, where the Stock Exchange and many international banks are.
4. Wall Street (very far downtown) •	• **d.** Where the World Trade Center used to be. The name comes from a military term for the spot where a bomb explodes.
5. United Nations headquarters (Midtown, East River) •	• **e.** A part of Fifth Avenue, about a mile long, next to Central Park, with major museums like The Met or the Guggenheim.
6. The Statue of Liberty •	• **f.** One of the tallest buildings in N.Y.C. From 1931 to 1971, it was the tallest in the world.

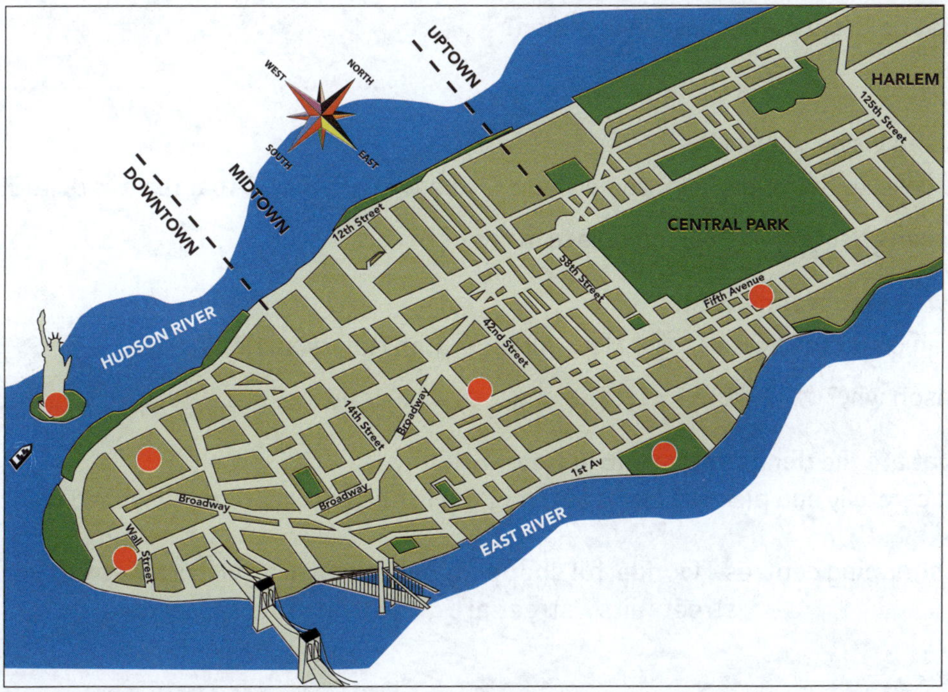

Manhattan

Activity 4 Listening to a New Yorker

MP3

A Group A **If you don't need help, take your notes as usual and get ready to recap information.**

B Group B **If you think you'll need some help, look at the following spidergram to help you take notes and prepare for recap.**

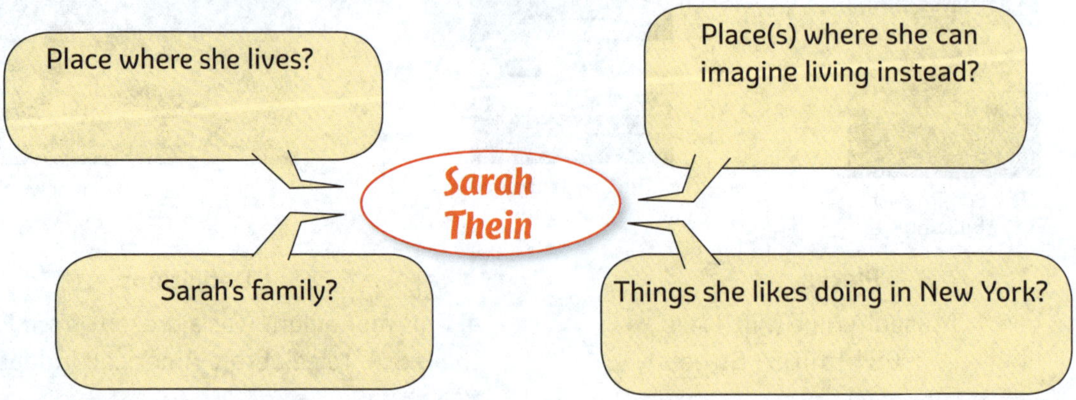

C Group C **If you think you'll need some more help, answer the following questions.**

1. Sarah Thein.

a. She grew up in ☐ Jackson's Light ☐ Jackson Heights ☐ 8, Jackson Street in ....

b. The borough where she grew up is the most ...., the most .... and the .... of the five boroughs.

2. List the places where Sarah would be ready to live apart from New York.

a. ....

b. ....

c. ....

3. What do these places have in common?

....

4. Sarah's vision of New York?

a. She believes that there is ☐ somewhere ☐ nowhere in the US that really is quite like New York.

b. It means New York is a unique place in terms of .... – it is ....

5. New Yorker or American?

a. Sarah considers herself ☐ a New Yorker ☐ an American first.

b. Reason why? ....

6. What are the things you can do in New York?

Listen carefully and pick out elements from the list below according to what Sarah says.

shopping centres • wonderful shopping galleries • art galleries • street vendors • street fairs • street art • museums • restaurants

7. Use all your answers to get ready to recap information.

Learn as You Wish

Getting a Feel for New York City

Memorise what you will need in Your Task. Choose the method you prefer, A or B.

A End-of-lesson Recapping

1. Review the whole worksheet. Feel free to use different colour highlighters to organise the new elements you have learned. You can also use the table or mind map below.

2. Rehearse with your partner. Tell him/her what you have learned about New York City and then it will be his/her turn. Do not hesitate to tell him/her what he/she forgot.

B Quiz about New York City

1. Review the whole worksheet. Feel free to use different colour highlighters to organise the new elements you have learned. You can also use the table or mind map below.

2. a. In pairs, invent 10 questions about New York City.

b. Each pair then ask one question to the other pairs (no information is available on the desks!)

What we learned:

History	Geography	Population	Places of interest	Famous people

Activity 5 Chain Speaking

The whole class is going to recap and every student, in his/her turn, has to give one piece of information about New York City really fast. If someone takes more than 5 seconds to think or repeats something that has already been said, they are out of the chain. Play until only one student is left or until the class has run out of things to say.

Your Task

Preparing a Short Talk

You are going to prepare a short talk about a NYC landmark or area you would like to visit. Join the profile that the teacher assigns you:

Group 1: Nature lovers: Central Park or the Bronx Zoo

Group 2: Shopaholics: Fifth Avenue or Times Square

Group 3: Museum goers: The Metropolitan Museum of Art or the Guggenheim

Group 4: Show business fans: Radio City or Gershwin Theater

Group 5: Young photographers: the Empire State Building or the Statue of Liberty

Group 6: History buffs: Ellis Island or the United Nations headquarters

1. @ CONNECT TO: collegien.nathan.fr/speak3

Check the website to make your choice between the two places. Be ready to explain your personal choice.

2. Students from each profile get together (one student with profile 1 + one with profile 2 + 1 with profile 3, etc.) and explain to one another where they want to go and why.

3. Each new group prepares a short PowerPoint presentation (with only a few slides) of the places they chose and they get ready to present their choice orally.

The article on page 73 can give you ideas for expressions, other places and activities.

This article can give you ideas for Your Task.

Taxi, MTA... or Sneakers?

The **MTA – Metropolitan Transit Authority** – runs the subway, buses and trains in New York and its surrounding areas. The subway will get you around the city quickly (and 24/7). But if you're looking for a more picturesque way to get from one place to another there are plenty of other options.

Hail a cab, a bright yellow New York taxi... though not during rush hour – at least not if you're in a hurry; or hop on a bus, making sure you have 'exact fare', take the bike track on the Brooklyn Bridge, or just slip into a pair of comfortable shoes or sneakers and discover the details that can only be seen by foot. From surprising street art to unexpected flora and fauna, you never know what you'll find...

You can spend days wandering the halls of great **museums** like the Guggenheim (modern art) or the Natural History Museum. There are also cosier ones, like the Frick Collection. Endless hours can also be spent lounging in the grass in Central Park with a book or some food and some friends, or if you're lucky you can take in a summer show or concert.

Some the best **restaurants** are ones that require nothing more than your fingers and a stack of napkins. For a quick bite to eat, grab a hot dog at Gray's Papaya in Hell's Kitchen, or find the hidden jewel at Le Parker Meridian called The Burger Joint.

NYC street food is are also pretty awesome if you're feeling adventurous. Street vendors and food carts are everywhere and super cheap too.

For a very different NYC experience, go to Standard Hotel's hip ping-pong club, SPiN New York. Great views over the Hudson River, breathtaking sunsets, ping-pong: what more could you ask for?

So no matter what your mood or your preference, the city's possibilities and combinations are endless. In fact, the best part of New York is being able to find just about anything, anytime, in "the city that never sleeps".

Activity 1 An Interview with the School's Careers Counsellor

Group B

You are the careers counsellor.

A Get ready to welcome Amber and prepare some questions to ask her to start the interview.

1. Identity? ....
2. Age? ....
3. Class? ....
4. GCSE* subjects? ....
5. Favourite subject(s)? ....
6. Hobbies? How often? ....
7. Future job? ....
8. Personality? ....

B Look at the following job card.

1. Get ready to answer Amber's questions.

2. Check that she understands all the tasks involved in being a chef:

You know that as a chef, you will have to... Chefs must...

Words

GCSE: General Certificate of Secondary Education – an exam taken by many British students at age 16

CHEFS

Description

Chefs plan menus and prepare, or supervise the preparation of food in hotels, restaurants, clubs...

Qualifications

You may not need any academic qualifications although it may help if you have GCSEs in subjects like English and maths.
There are certificates and diplomas but apprenticeship is also a good way to become a chef. On average, 2-to-4 years training is required before being considered a chef.

Tasks

- Buying food and checking quality.
- Planning menus, preparing meals or supervising their preparation.
- Supervising, organising and instructing kitchen staff and managing the whole kitchen.
- Ensuring hygiene, health and safety standards.
- Planning and co-ordinating kitchen work such as fetching, clearing and cleaning of equipment and utensils.

Starting Salary: £13,000 a year
Average Salary: £25,480 a year
Average Weekly Hours: 43
Unemployment: 8%

Gender Balance:

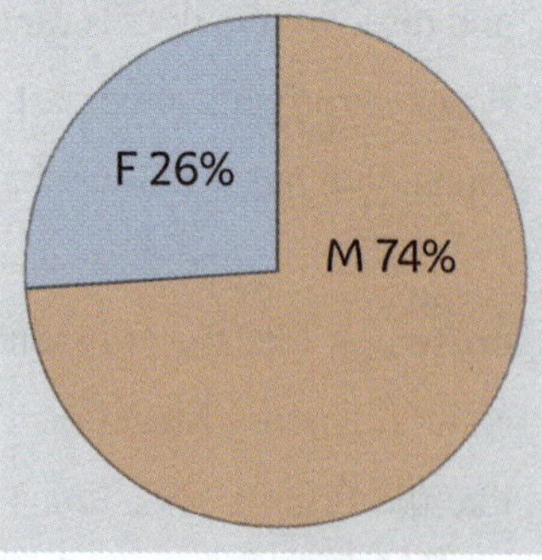

C Give Amber some advice.

do some training periods in restaurants • get a week's work experience in a professional kitchen • try and find a job in a restaurant during the holidays...

You should/shouldn't... If I were you, I would... Why don't you...?

D Pair up with someone from the other group and practise your interview for five minutes. Get ready to perform it in front of the class.

@ CONNECT TO: collegien.nathan.fr/speak3 to discover other careers.

Activity 3 Sherlock Holmes Webquest

Group B

A @ CONNECT TO: collegien.nathan.fr/speak3

Read the first two paragraphs. Get ready to answer the other group's questions about Joseph Bell:

1. Period when he lived?

....

2. Reasons for fame at the time? today?

....

3. Job(s)?

....

4. Person he was influenced by?

....

5. Examples of his deductions?

....

6. People's reaction?

....

7. Impact on his practice as a doctor?

....

B **Use the following prompts to ask the other group questions about Sir Arthur Conan Doyle.**

1. His activity? ....

2. Other books he wrote apart from Sherlock Holmes stories?

....

3. Event that occurred in 1893? ....

4. People's reaction? ....

5. Information about his family? ....

6. Place of residence in England? ....

7. Other hobbies or interests? ....

Activity 1 William Shakespeare

Group B

A **What was going on in the world while Shakespeare was writing and performing his plays?**

@ CONNECT TO: collegien.nathan.fr/speak3

First timeline: Click on "the 1500s" (the fifteen hundreds). Concentrate on the period between 1553-1599 and find the following information:

1. Monarch in England until 1603: ....

2. Monarch in France: ....

3. European presence in North America: ....

B **Second timeline: click on "the 1600s" in the dark blue box at the top of the page.**

1. Monarch in England (Careful, this piece of information is not explicitly mentioned, you have to use your power of deduction!): ....

2. Name of another major writer and his world-famous book: ....

3. Major scientific discovery which changed the way people saw the world:

....

4. English presence in North America: ....

C **Get ready to tell the other group about Shakespeare's time, and to take notes about their presentation. Read "Learn as You Wish" on p. 21 for some tips!**

Notes

....

....

....

....

....

....

....

....

....

Activity 2 Listening to a conversation

Group B

MP3 **B** **Listen to Part 2, complete and get ready to report.**

1. Select the picture that corresponds best and pick out words to prove your point.

a ☐

b ☐

c ☐

....

....

2. Select the right adjectives and get ready to give more details about the sculpture.

enormous • wooden • metallic • true • blue • green • pink • shiny • Chinese • Polish • polished • brilliant • curved • curvy • carved

3. Effect? Select the correct picture and pick out words to prove your point.

a ☐

b ☐

c ☐

4. Get ready to report.

Activity 1 Reading about New York's Five Boroughs

Pupil B

A **Read about Brooklyn and Staten Island.**

Unique New York

New York is a cultural melting pot of people of different races, ethnicities, religions, points of view and professions. With great street food and street theatres, museums, art galleries and Broadway theatres, restaurants, shopping and parks, New York has something for everyone.

Times Square and Manhattan skyscrapers.

"The City" — as any self-respecting New Yorker calls it — is made up of five boroughs, which were designated in 1898: Manhattan, Brooklyn, Queens, The Bronx, and Staten Island.

Brooklyn

Brooklyn, south of Queens and Manhattan, is now one of the trendiest and most attractive areas for young New Yorkers to live, eat and play. It is also one of the most ethnically diverse parts of the city, home to African-Americans, Orthodox and Hassidic Jews, Italian-Americans, Hispanics, Russians, West Indians, Irish and more. There's plenty to see and do in Brooklyn, from visiting the N.Y. Aquarium or doing some vintage shopping in Williamsburg to catching a music, dance or theatre performance at BAM (the Brooklyn Academy of Music) or going to the funfair and beach at Coney Island.

Go to the funfair and beach in the city on Coney Island.

Be like a New Yorker, not a tourist. Take the Staten Island ferry to the Statue of Liberty.

Staten Island

The celebrated wedding scene in *The Godfather* was shot on location on Staten Island, as were some street scenes in *Goodfellas*. That speaks volumes about the least-populated borough's reputation. But today it's a middle-class area, more *Desperate Housewives* than Mafia! Residents commute to work in Manhattan by ferry (there's no subway to Staten Island, which is physically connected to Brooklyn and New Jersey by bridges only. New Yorkers from other boroughs like to joke about never having set foot on Staten Island. That is their loss, because the island is an oasis of tranquillity, and the ferry ride is one of the best bargains in the city, offering splendid views of downtown Manhattan and the Statue of Liberty for a fraction of the price (and waiting time) of the ferry to Liberty Island.

B **Locate the two boroughs you read about on the map and ask your partner questions to find the other three.**

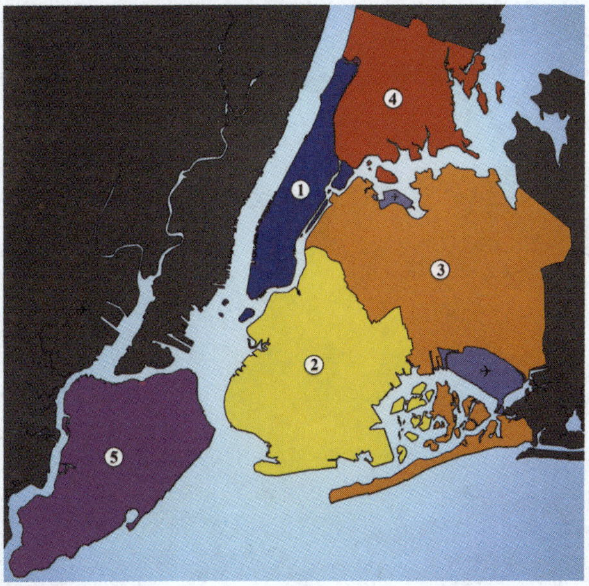

1. ....
2. ....
3. ....
4. ....
5. ....

MP3 **C** **Listen to check your answers and practise the pronunciation of the place names.**

D **Ask your partner questions to complete the information on the population chart. How many...? How big...?**

The five boroughs' area and population:

Brooklyn		2,567,000
The Bronx		1,397,000
Manhattan	59 km²	
Queens		2,300,000
Staten Island	151 km²	

Crédits photographiques

4 ht d ISTOCK/Mikolette ; **7** LACORS ; **8** THINKSTOCK/Nick White **9 ht** CHRISTOPHE L COLLECTION/ BBC TV ; **10** Visitbritain **11 ht** KHARBINE-TAPABOR/British Library ; **15** Peace Corps ; **18 ht** GETTY IMAGES France/Bettmann ; **19** Peace Corps ; **20 bas d** SIPA PRESS/AP ; **20 bas g** REUTERS (Thomson-Reuters)/ ; **21** DR ; **22 h** Linda Nylind/Shakespeare's Globe ; **22 h** THINKSTOCK ; **25** DR ; **28** SHUTTERSTOCK/O Driscoll Imaging ; **31** ISTOCK/ ChristopherFutcher ; **35 h g** SHUTTERSTOCK/Tsekhmister **h m** SHUTTERSTOCK **h d** SHUTTERSTOCK/HandmadePictures **m g** SHUTTERSTOCK/marco meyer **m m** SHUTTERSTOCK/zkruger **m d** SHUTTERSTOCK/SEAGULL_L **bas g** SHUTTERSTOCK/Nataliia Pyzhova **bas d** SHUTTERSTOCK/Peter O'Toole ; **38** SHUTTERSTOCK/Joe Gough ; **39** Visitbritain ; **40 ht** GETTY IMAGES France/Waywood Maggee ; **40 bas** GETTY IMAGES France/ Daily Herald Archive ; **42 ht** GETTY IMAGES France/Worldwide Photography/Heritage Images/Paul Walters ; **45** Visitbritain ; **46 h** DREAMSTIME/Clive Chilvers **b** Visitbritain **49 haut d** LA COLLECTION/Artothek/ Christie's © Estate of Roy Lichtenstein New York / ADAGP Paris 2016 ; **48 bas g** SIPA PRESS/Kirsty Wigglesworth © The Andy Warhol Foundation for the Visual Arts, INC / ADAGP Paris 2016 ; **52 g** CHINENOUVELLE/SIPA © Jeff Koons **d** BRIDGEMAN IMAGES/ Scottish National gallery Edinburgh ; **54** European Union ; **56** European Union ; **58** IWM ; **61** National Theatre ; **62** Michael Morpurgo ; **63** Egmont ; **66** NYC&Co **67** NYC&Co **68** Rue des Archives **69** NYC&Co; **72** NYC&Co ; **73** NYC&Co; **74** ISTOCK/Mikolette ; **76** DR ; **78** NYC&Co **ht g** SHUTTERSTOCK/ Venturelli Luca ; **79** NYC&Co.

N° d'éditeur : 10222795 - Mai 2016
Achevé d'imprimer en France par l'imprimerie Clerc